MONEY LEAKS

The 5 secrets for entrepreneurs to take charge of their money leaks and attain financial freedom, irrespective of their current income

MONEY LEAKS

The 5 secrets for entrepreneurs to take charge of their money leaks and attain financial freedom, irrespective of their current income

Ganesan T

Copyright © 2018 Ganesan T

All the information, techniques, ideas, and concepts contained in this publication are general comments only and are not in any way recommended as individual advice. The intent is to offer a variety of information to provide a wide range of choices, now and in future, recognizing that we all have widely diverse circumstances and viewpoints. Should any reader choose to make use of the information contained herein, it is solely the reader's decision. Contributors (and their companies), authors, and publishers do not assume any responsibility whatsoever under any conditions or circumstances. It is recommended that readers obtain their own, independent financial advice.

Title: *Money Leaks*
Author: *Ganesan T*

Publisher: Success Gyan Publishing
A division of Success Gyan India Pvt. Ltd.
Old no:30 New no:24, Bhagirathi Ammal St,
T.Nagar, Chennai-600017
www.sgpublication.com

LIMITS OF LIABILITY/DISCLAIMER OF WARRANTY: The author and publisher of this book have used their best efforts in preparing this material. The author and publisher disclaim any warranties (expressed or implied), or merchantability for any particular purpose. The author and publisher shall in no event be held liable for any loss or other damages, including, but not limited to special, incidental, consequential, or other damages. The information presented in this publication is compiled from sources believed to be accurate at the time of printing, however, the publisher assumes no responsibility for errors or omissions. The information in this publication is not intended to replace or substitute professional advice. The author and publisher specifically disclaim any liability, loss, or risk that is incurred as a consequence, directly or indirectly, of the use and application of any of the contents of this information.

Success Gyan Publishing bears no responsibility for the accuracy of information on any websites cited and/or used by the author in this book. The inclusion of website addresses in this book does not constitute an endorsement by, or associate Success Gyan Publishing with such sites or the content, products, advertising or other materials presented.

Opinions expressed by the author do not necessarily represent the views and opinions of Success Gyan Publishing. The publisher assumes no liability for any content or opinion expressed by, or through the author.

Printed in India

To my dad, mom, and brother
who have been my source of strength through the years.

Table of Contents

Foreword 9

Acknowledgements 13

Introduction 15

Expenses and Savings

Chapter 1: Life As It Is 19

Chapter 2: Accepting Your Today 31

Chapter 3: Take Your First Step 43

Insurance

Chapter 4: Securing Your Life 53

Investment

Chapter 5: Tomorrow's Essential 65

Chapter 6: Various Ways 77

Chapter 7: How to Choose? 91

Loans

Chapter 8: Outstanding Life 107

Lifestyle

Chapter 9: Life with Style... 119

Chapter 10: Your Money Matters 127

Final Summary 135

Interviews... 137

Free Bonus: Download your "Action Guide" for FREE 147

About Success Gyan Publishing.. 149

Foreword

The predominant message in our culture is that it's all about the money. We believe that more money or a different set of financial circumstances will bring us the freedom to stop worrying and just enjoy life.

But many people are stuck in the same financial predicament even though they've tried everything they know to get ahead. No matter what your balance sheet looks like, you already suspect that there has to be a way to make the lasting, profound changes that you crave in your financial life. You wouldn't have picked up this book otherwise.

One reason most people aren't happy with their financial lives is the way we have traditionally been taught to deal with money, which simply doesn't work.

We are told to spend less, save more, think positive thoughts that will create the abundance we want, or find the perfect career. We set goals, create budgets, put all the right insurance in place, write updated wills and estate plans, and invest in a certain way.

When it comes to money, most of us have experienced one or more of the following:

- Feelings of anxiety and fear
- A sense that money is separate from the more sacred or spiritual parts of our lives
- Endless wants or the feeling that we'll never have enough money to be happy
- Frustration with a spouse or family member regarding spending habits

The belief that our finances are beyond our control.

The source of all change and all possibility is becoming aware of the limitation that we have chosen.

We earn lots of money and check how much money we have earned from the time we started earning. Are you still holding all the millions you earned?

Our self-programmed, unconscious habits have guided us to siphon all the money into unnecessary things in our life. One fine day, we realize that in spite of all the hard work these many years, we have a negligible bank balance.

FOREWORD

This book, written by Ganesan, is full of possibilities on how we can change our inner thinking and beliefs about money, how we can arrest the money leakage in our life and lead a wealthy and prosperous life.

This book is more like a workbook, and you need to work this book in your daily life.

My best wishes to all the readers, and I hope you apply the learnings from this book in life to bring about profound transformation in your money beliefs, money habits, and the way you spend, save, and invest money for your loved ones.

Joyfully yours,
Murali Sundaram
Happyness Coach, Author, and Philosopher
www.HappynessCoach.co.in

"If you are an individual with a quest to explore a lifestyle with financial freedom or an entrepreneur who wishes to ensure a steady source of personal income to safeguard one's family's wellbeing irrespective of the ups and downs in the business side of the income then this is a must read. This book provides you with a fundamental and systemic approach to money management that will inspire you to solve the challenges with your financial wellbeing. Ganesan T has cracked the code and brings to the table an action guide that enables you to manage money in the short and long terms effectively. I highly recommend this book due to the author's approach to breaking complicated financial concepts to a comprehensive step-by-step guide for anyone who is looking to better their lives by attaining financial freedom."

Owner: Sriram Subramanya
Founder, Managing Director, and CEO

INTEGRA SOFTWARE SERVICES PRIVATE LIMITED
100 Feet Road (ECR), Pakkamudiyanpet,
Pondicherry 605 008, India

Acknowledgements

It has been a dream come true to write this book and get it published. Now I truly believe that if you want something in your life, it will come true because of incredible people. All you need is big dreams and the belief that it will happen.

Here are some incredible people who helped getting my dream book published.

My mom, Valarmathi, and brother, Baranikumar, who stood by my entrepreneurial journey all these years.

Murali Sundaram, who helped me complete the book. If there was any problem, he was always there to make it simpler.

I would like to thank Surendran, a man of few words and a great mission. He made things easier while writing this book with the support of his great team. He also helped getting the book published.

Thanks to my editorial team—Jyotsna, Sushmita, and Claudia. Your efforts at transforming my first draft into a complete book have been commendable.

I would like to thank everyone who has been part of this journey of reaching out to millions of people and helping them attain financial freedom.

Introduction

Do you feel like you need to work for money until your last breath?

How many times have you just procrastinated with the thought of investing for a long time just because of your current income?

This book is written for the millions of people who want to structure their personal financial life and get their own financial freedom.

Money Leaks contains five secret steps, which can help you in creating wealth irrespective of your income. Your wealth creation does not depend on the income you are generating at the moment. All you need to do is follow these five steps diligently. You can achieve your desired lifestyle easily and can create wealth for yourself.

Through this book, I am not only sharing my experience but also the combined wisdom of entrepreneurs who had made it big in the industry and created wealth for themselves too. They were clear in their business plans. In their personal life, they took the steps necessary to achieve their desired lifestyle.

The steps shared here will help you in creating wealth in the long term and come out of your debt. It will help you avoid costly investment mistakes and needed risk management measures. The five leaks if arrested can surely help in creating wealth for yourself. All five leaks need to be checked upon in order to create wealth.

Raghukumar of Sekaram Associates and Srinivasan of Mother designers have followed the steps suggested in this book to realign their financial priorities in their life. They are currently not worried about their personal finance as everything is in order for them to reach their financial goals.

I promise you that it is easy for you to do it. By following the step-by-step process, you can attain financial freedom. Financial freedom is nothing but not worrying about money even if you quit your business right now. In less than a month of implementing these steps, you can bring in money and happiness into your life. Some may need to start saving first, some may need to start closing their debts as first step, some may need to manage their risk in their life as first step, some may need to start investing as first step, and some may need to enjoy their lifestyle with their money. I assure you that you will take the first step as per your financial life after reading this book.

Don't wait for the next level of growth in your business. Don't get carried away by your biases. Accept your reality. Your money life depends on your actions. Check out the five common leaks, which will happen in anyone's life. It may be expenses and savings, insurance, investments, loans, and lifestyle. Choose which one you need to focus on and start working on that area. You need to lead a life where you are not worried about money anymore. Join me as I take you through your journey in achieving financial freedom.

At this point, you have a choice. You can either doubt your ability to earn more, or take massive actions with your current income and achieve everything in your life. All you need is self-belief and to take the actions that can bring in wealth in your life. You can either flip through this book like just another personal finance book, or you can treat it like workbook and take an action after every chapter. The choice is yours.

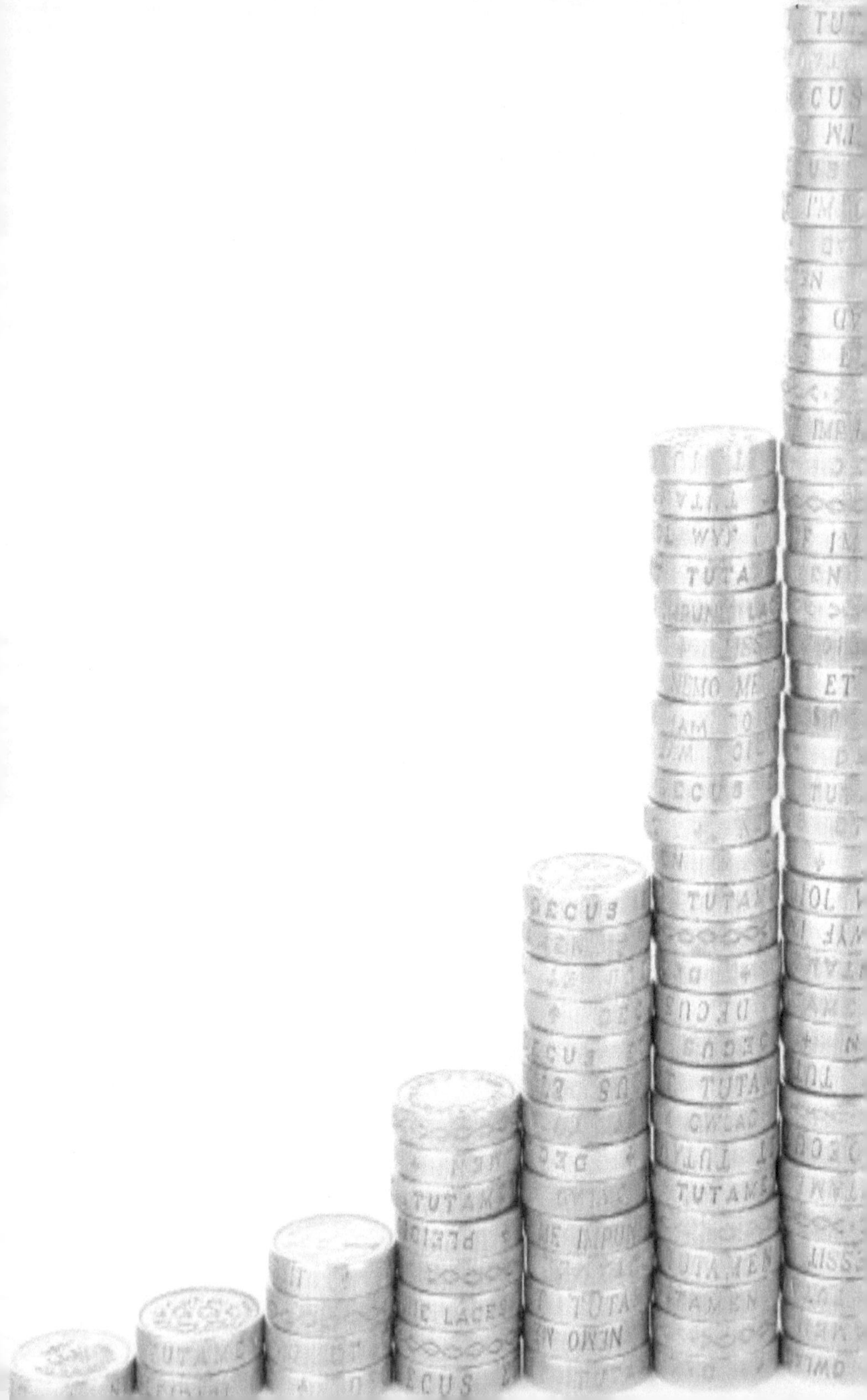

CHAPTER 1

Life As It Is

Money is the one and only thing, which differentiates everyone in this world.

Money differentiates everyone in this world. Life with money can be happier with loved ones. We have moved on from living in a village to urban areas because of facilities like better schooling for kids with nearby hospitals, and better income to take care of the family. Each one of us wishes to have a better lifestyle now.

One thing that has become a part of everyone's life is EMI. Yes, this helped many enjoy their daily life and also made everyone's life easy. In particular, this EMI made everything that was a distant dream for many, become a part of everyone's life. Two decades ago, a person who had a television was considered a rich person.

All these essentials increased the expenses in each family in the last ten years.

Have you noticed?

How many times have you tried saving an amount of money and ended up saying, "Let me see next month, when my financial condition improves."

"Tomorrow never dies, so start saving now."

Tomorrow Never Dies is one of my favorite James Bond movies. I remember this quote whenever I am spending a lot and not saving. If you need to save, just say to yourself, "Tomorrow never dies, so start saving now."

Best example for everyone to understand this impact is the mobile. It has brought the whole world into our hands. There is no doubt about this fact. I still remember my first mobile that I bought in 2006. It cost around INR 2000 and was usually recharged for few hundred rupees a month. Once I joined my corporate career, my first mobile was Nokia. In another two years, I bought Sony for INR 10,000. Then from 2011, I started buying premium mobiles for around INR 30,000. This expense has slowly crept into everyone's family.

Mobiles have become one essential expense, which you need to spend on once in two or three years. There are reports that say that a few people change their mobiles even once in a year.

Peer pressure

Once you start generating income, slowly you will start seeing the world. You can start splurging on things that you were expecting to do once you start earning. A vacation along with your friends. Airbnb and all other tourism industries have made flying simpler. You even get packages at cheaper rates to explore the world.

Most of the lifestyle expenses may be due to peer pressure unknowingly. Just look around your living room. How many things you have that is of no use now.

For example, a simple LED TV would have cost around INR 30,000 only. As you watched the Smart TV in your friend's house, you too decided to invest in the same, which is around INR 75,000. I am not denying the fact that this Smart TV gives you a host of benefits but do you really need this at the moment in your life?

Necessity is the mother of invention. Similarly, "EMI is the mother of all expenses" as it eases the need to have the money to buy something. Credit cards have eased repayment to a great level. Basic necessities in life are shelter and food. This basic need forced people to earn and lead a life. Now the "must have" tag is etched upon luxury items, forcing people to spend on these things. Each and everything in life has "*Must have*" tag line nowadays.

How to control your expenses?

Now it is evident that you spend a lot. Expenses are inevitable. These expenses increase with every rise in income.

"Income increase leads to expense increase"

Do you remember your first income?

What is your last month's income?

How many times has your income increased since you started working?

What is your average monthly expense for your family five years back?

What is your average monthly expense in the last month?

First step to control expenses is to prepare a list before going shopping. Also, prepare a list of big purchases in the next two or three months. Online e-commerce portals started offering discounts once in a quarter, and some offline stores offer discounts even on a monthly basis.

All you need to do is wait for a while until you go and buy these big ticket items.

All expenses are essential in this world. There should always be a strong *why* behind everything you do. Cutting down expenses today can help spend on your tomorrow's essential expenses. These are your "why reasons" or goals. If you are a married person, the general goals can be as below:

1. Kid's education
2. Kid's marriage
3. Retirement

Apart from this, there can be many other goals that will help you in saving. There is popular saying, "Little drops make a mighty ocean."

So start small first and then you can make your money count for you. All these years, people who didn't even think about savings have started saving from their monthly income. They have even increased their investment amount over a period of time.

Importance of finding goals

Rahul started his own business five years back. He has developed his company slowly and steadily. He has been withdrawing a specific amount per month. He has also made sure that he withdraws a bonus from his company every year out of the profits. He was able to achieve his business target in the last five years. He is clear in his business goals.

In his personal life, he bought his home and rented it out. He has been living in a rented home near his office. He did the income and expense self-analysis in his life. Apart from the house that he bought on a loan, nothing exists. Finally, he started investing for his kids' education as the first step.

Emergency fund

Whenever you plan to make an investment, some emergency situation may arise out of the blue, which will force you to postpone everything. An ideal way to start planning is to identify your monthly expenses. Keep six months expenses as emergency fund. This has to be always available for you. You need to keep it liquid.

In each stage of life, there are some essential things that you need to do.

In your twenties, you would have started earning and indulge in spending money the most.

In your thirties, by the time you realize that you are spending a lot, you would be married. This will further increase your monthly expenses. This is the time around which you need to buy a home as well. It may be a dream or pressure from a parent, but you need to buy this asset.

In your forties, your income would have increased by now, but you would have focused only on closing the home loans and other existing loans.

In your fifties, you may need to start focusing on your retirement plan.

In your sixties, this is the distribution phase where your accumulated assets can be slowly distributed until you die.

If you look at each stage of life, there will be some big expense that will force you to postpone your savings and investments.

Importance of the emergency fund

Monthly expenses of Sridhar were INR 50,000, and he has been running a waste management organization for the last seven years. He has been travelling extensively, and money was never an issue for him in the last seven years. He along with his brother has been planning to buy a duplex home and stay together for a longer period. After settling down in Chennai, he had agreed to his brother's idea.

They had arranged a down payment of 10 lakhs and their EMI was going to start soon. They didn't manage to hold onto any emergency funds. All of a sudden, his father got a heart-related ailment, and the doctors advised them to do an operation at the earliest. His father is seventy and doesn't have health insurance. He was completely stressed as he has not asked for money from anyone until now. Finally, one of his friends gave him the required amount.

What he could have done differently?

His monthly expense - INR 50,000

Emergency corpus - (four to six) month expenses

So ideally, he should have had a minimum of two to three lakhs in his bank account as fixed deposit or liquid mutual fund.

Another option is that his father should have had health insurance.

Average expense

I used to discuss the importance of savings and investments with my friends. Whenever I start, one of the guys would say that he had a lot of EMIs to close. He is a marine engineer by profession and during the sailing period, he earns a lot in dollars. This has been going on for the last two or three years.

One day, I asked him to list down the EMIs and the other expenses he had. In the next two minutes, he listed all the big EMIs. After that, he has been complaining about his father for his careless spending. Then I asked him, if he was noting it down in a notebook or an app to track his daily expense. The obvious answer was no. This has been the case for most of you. You will not include miscellaneous expenses, but this will be the big hole in your monthly cash flow analysis.

Another friend of mine notes down each and every expense he makes in a notebook on a daily basis. This clearly shows how your expense has increased in the last few years.

List down your known monthly expense now. Then go deeper in the next month by noting down every expense. Do it for one more month. Now you can know your average monthly expense. I can strongly vouch that it would have given you a picture of how much unwanted expenditures you are making.

> *"Do not save what is left after spending, but spend what is left after saving"*
> *- Warren Buffet*

Warren Buffet summed it up beautifully in this quote. Spend only what is left after saving.

Roy used to pay off monthly bills on time during the first week of the month, once he gets his income. After fifteen days, he will start using his credit card for any purchases. This has been his monthly routine. He never lived on debts and whenever he purchased something in debt, he would close it as soon as possible. If someone asks about any savings or investments, he will share all his details. Looking at this everyone will feel pity. One thing to note down here is that he is paying his bills in the first week of every month. He got a credit card to spend on his expenses for rest of the month.

Credit cards provide a credit limit until which you can purchase any goods. Therefore, you can continue spending until that limit is reached. Roy can never get out of this rat race. He can make a small change, which is nothing but paying bills at the end of the month or saving something for himself as the first step.

In the following month, Roy decided to save 10 percent of his income in a separate bank account. Then he continued his monthly expenses using the card. This month he was careful with his expenditure, as he knew that he needs to save again from the next month's income also, and so he cannot utilize his entire credit limit. During the next month, he had paid a lesser credit card bill compared to the previous month.

After a year, he was able to save a minimum of 20 percent of his income. All savings cannot happen overnight, it takes careful planning over a period of time.

Summary

1. "Tomorrow never dies, so do it now" - to control your expenses and make savings now
2. Income vs. expense - self-analyze to understand that income increases with expense
3. Finding a goal can help in cutting down expenses
4. Having an emergency fund can help you with regular savings
5. Find out the average expense of your family
6. Slowly try to increase your savings to 30 percent of your income

Action points

1. Your Income in this month -
2. Your Expense in this month -
3. Your Savings in this month -
4. How much percentage did you save - (Savings or Income)
5. Your Emergency fund -

For cutting down your expenses:

1. Start saving 10 percent
2. Make your Expense list for this month and do within that limit
3. Target or goal - 30 percent savings over a period of six months

CHAPTER 2

Accepting Your Today

> *"It's only when the tide goes out that you discover who's been swimming naked."*
> *- Warren Buffet*

He had quoted this for identifying the best stocks in the stock market. When there is Bull Run in the stock market, all the stocks keep rising. Only when the bull stops, you know which stock is safe to hold on too. If you ask me, this is suitable for every individual at any point of time. I have discovered this truth when I did this exercise with one of my relatives. He had big assets, a home in Chennai without a loan. He had started investing in mutual funds regularly, and he gets a big paycheck every month.

He had a few aspirations like going on a vacation every year, education for his kid, etc. As his income was on the higher end, he didn't worry about all these aspirations. He didn't think about retiring early or starting his own business.

Slowly when I shared about the necessity of having long-term goals and regular investments to achieve that, he opened up and started understanding his reality. His situation is not alarming, but it needs to be addressed, as he had a dependent wife and a kid to take care of, in his absence.

Like this, do a self-analysis on your life.

Do you have clear plan for the next five years, until your retirement and thereafter?

Do you know clearly about your monthly cash flows?

Do you know if your investments will take care of you, during your retirement period?

Do you discuss with your partner regarding your financial positions?

All these questions may come to your mind occasionally, but you will ignore it.

The ultimate reason is, that it needs serious introspection and your inner voice will say,

"Please ignore and you have a lot of other work to do."

Everybody in his or her life will be influenced. The first influencer in everyone's life is his or her mother. Followed by the father and relatives, neighbors, friends, etc. As life progresses, all these experiences will have a bigger impact on their financial decisions.

Rahul had a successful entrepreneurial life, and he is one of the richest people in his locality. His family attended all social gatherings. Once, while staying at a hotel, his son had given a tip of INR 2000. He, in his room, had given a tip of INR 100. Out of curiosity, the room boy had enquired with him directly. Rahul politely replied that he is the son of a clerk, and his son is the father of a rich entrepreneur.

In some of the cases, even though you are not interested in spending, due to peer pressure you end up spending a lot of money. This is purely because you don't want to lose your friends.

The point to note here is that, the upbringing and influence play a major role in the way you deal with money. Respect your money and the way it is playing a major role in your life. If you are spending it on useless things, then automatically the fortune finds its way out.

First step is to understand reality and accept it.

If you are spending a lot, acknowledge that.

If you are a miser, acknowledge the fact.

Now you will be able to find the shift in asset growth in your life over a period of time.

Biases

Sometimes it is difficult to identify if you are influenced, or biased. Influence refers to any good qualities directly inherited from a person. Biases can be an inclination toward, or a prejudice on something. I developed a bias of going against my father's wishes on investing in equities. He goes for safety and secure investing, while I invested in equities. This happened when I started my career.

There are different types of biases. Please check if you can identify your biases among these:

1. Anchoring or confirmation bias
2. Regret aversion bias
3. Disposition effect bias
4. Hindsight bias
5. Familiarity bias
6. Self-attribution bias
7. Trend chasing bias
8. Worry

Anchoring bias

It is hard to break the belief of some people. They try to find everything positive related to their beliefs and they ignore the rest. I have seen many people (without even trying to understand the stock markets) directly jump to the conclusion that the stock market is risky.

Another example is when people think that savings and investments are for those people who earn a lot of money. Savings and investment can be started at any point of time in your life.

Do you have an anchoring bias?

Loss aversion bias
Some people will never set expectations in their life. The ultimate reason usually is that they don't want to be disappointed in life if their expectations are not met.

Loans can sometimes help you in creating assets. Take the case of owning a home. It is an asset for life. You may not think about taking a loan that is beyond your comfort zone. One of my friends bought a two BHK flat for few lakhs while he ideally wanted a three BHK flat. He could have got the three BHK flat with his income, as he was eligible. The reason for buying the two BHK flat is that he was not willing to go beyond his comfort level of paying the EMI.

Do you have a loss aversion bias?

Disposition effect bias

Are you judgmental?

ULIP was sold in a wrong way during 2007–2008. ULIP is an insurance plus investment product which invests in stock market also. Many didn't understand this point. Most of them lost money during 2007–2008 because stock market had fallen by more than 50 percent and their ULIP value also fallen drastically. To control this, insurance regulator has taken series of steps till now.

Still many do not opt for ULIP because of the effect it had created.

Do you have a disposition effect bias?

Hindsight bias

Most stock analysts will make predictions based on the past data. In most of the situations, it may be short-term predictions, which may or may not work.

In the case of the monsoon, the past data may not hold true on whether this year monsoon will get set during the same period. Even 100 percent rainfall cannot be predicted due to so many factors.

Do you have a hindsight bias?

Familiarity bias

This happens when you are familiar with a product. Real estate would have given you substantial returns in the past decade. Based on that if you invest your money, it may not yield bigger returns in the next five years. Ultimately, the market conditions, government regulations, and many such factors play an important role in the price change.

Do you have a familiarity bias?

Self-attribution bias

When you start handling money and taking financial decisions you will feel like you are confident.

During positive outcomes, you will attribute it to your decision-making abilities and during negative outcomes you attribute it to external factors.

Do you have a self-attribution bias?

Trend chasing bias

This bias can lead to huge losses. Take the recent example in 2018, when the price of Bitcoin started increasing and everyone became so confident that it is the future currency.

After a couple of months, many countries started banning that digital currency. This led to a huge fall from $20,000 to $6000 now. Whoever invested lost huge amount of money.

Do you have any trend chasing bias?

Worry

If you are worried by the fact that there is "risk" in an investment, then it may be a bias. Risk is there in all parts of life—from the time you sleep and until the time you open your eyes the next morning. No one is sure of his or her existence.

The best thing to do is to stop worrying about everything and look at what is good for your life. Though this is not a bias, worrying will impact your investment decisions.

Do you have worry when it comes to money?

How to avoid these biases?

You need to acknowledge the fact that you have certain biases. Let us see some of the steps that can help you in identifying your biases:

1. Accept that you may have some biases
2. Look at the pattern of your investments
3. Check if you seek opinions to support your views
4. Check if you seek opinions about investing
5. Check if you worry whenever your investment is going down
6. Check if you judge others opinions on certain products

Once you do step one and two, see which category you are falling under. Once you identify it, the easier it is to overcome it.

If you don't have any biases, it is easy to listen or learn from others and multiply your wealth.

One of the easy options is going to an expert. In the case of wealth accumulation, approaching a financial advisor is the best way. This is an information world. If you Google, there is a lot of information available to understand and decide on how to work with your finances.

If you are someone who doesn't have time, it is best to approach a financial advisor or a consultant.

"Most people need a planner. The ones who don't need one are usually smart enough to use one"
- Loren Dunton

Rajesh has been running a business for the last twenty-five years. In his investment pattern, whenever he accumulated a surplus amount from his business, he used to buy a piece of land across the city. He also has been investing in an ULIP policy for the last nine years. His son got a seat in a reputed university in Singapore. He never expected this to happen. He thought a college in India might be the first preference and planned his finances accordingly. Now with this huge opportunity for his son, he wants to fund the education in Singapore. He couldn't sell any of his physical assets as there was no immediate buyer and the money needed to be managed immediately. Finally, he sold his ULIP. He was happy with the returns it had generated in the last nine years. I enquired about the investment amount and the total value he got back while closing. The total returns it generated was not even 8 percent. Considering the inflation, the returns were negligible.

He was shocked to see the returns percentage. Finally, he came to the conclusion to invest more in financial assets and taking care of the liquidity needs.

Summary

1. Why me and why now - accept your reality
2. Find your biases in your life
3. How to avoid these biases

Action points

1. Do a self-analysis of your financial life and accept your reality.
2. Identify your bias.
3. Avoid bias, learn, and implement what is needed for your financial life.
4. Simply approach a financial advisor for better life.

CHAPTER 3

Take Your First Step

"A penny saved is a penny earned"
- *Benjamin Franklin*

Savings need not be done separately. Even a rupee saved is a rupee earned. I was attending one of the training programs where the speaker had turned his focus to increasing financial habits and making a fortune with a live example. He has been in the industry for the last twenty-five years and everyone knew him as a veteran. So the audience was keen to listen to every bit of his speech.

We were having the training in a big hall and there was no one seated at the back. He observed that we could consider saving INR10 an hour by shutting down the ACs and lights at the back. For a day, the saving may be close to INR 100 and in thirty days, you may end saving INR 3000. Out of thin air, INR 3000 had been saved in a month. This would have been an unwanted expense. This is applicable in business, so check your monthly cash flow. Analyze it every month. Surely, you can improve something over a period of time.

In your life, what is the one thing you can switch off and save something?

Savings as per GDP

India has one of the healthiest savings ratio as the percentage of GDP is at around 32 percent. China has a ratio of 46 percent, while the United States is around 18 percent of the GDP. This plays a crucial role. It is arrived at by deducting the consumer expenditure from the total savings. In the last few years, people slowly shifted toward financial assets instead of physical assets. Physical assets didn't generate enough returns and overall growth of equity across the world, forcing people to turn toward financial assets.

After independence, India slowly started getting into the path of development. Much of the economic growth happened only after the liberalization policies that were announced in 1991. Slowly there has been a shift in the consumer behavior over the last decade.

Many household women who had saved in the form of INR 500 and INR 1000 notes found it difficult to exchange their notes during demonetization. Many families literally had lakhs of money as their savings for so many years. They had saved it at home in case of an emergency.

More than earning lots of money, it is how much you save for your life that matters the most.

Savings in present situation

Taking cue from the previous chapter it is easy to say that savings is difficult in the present situation. Ultimately, the thing that can improve your life is savings.

Difficulties in saving:

- Credit card bill
- Dependents
- Monthly groceries
- Mobile bills
- Broadband and Internet
- Personal grooming
- Other EMIs

If you see, the first point has been left blank. Ideally, difficulty in saving should come on top of this list. Now you know the first difficulty itself is the mindset of saving and the rest are all reasons. One valid reason which can help you in saving is finding the *why* as mentioned in the previous chapter.

Another important reason is inflation. Inflation is nothing but the increase in the price of goods. Consumer inflation in India has always touched double digits and from 2017, it started coming down. India has been a major importer of crude oil and gold. Foreign exchange and the price of crude oil are all external factors, which cannot be controlled in India.

From the late 1960s, the inflation started rising and the average inflation rate has been around 8 percent in the last few decades. For example, if the price of a product is INR 100 and the inflation for a year is around 8 percent. Then the price of this product by next year will be around INR 108. This forced banks to have fixed deposit rates to be higher than inflation percentage. We didn't have any expenses apart from the basic needs of our family. Therefore, bank fixed deposit rates itself created a fortune for a person who has been saving regularly. Remember that there were no other big expenses in those years. Education was available at a nominal price.

Now along with consumer inflation, there is education inflation, medical inflation, etc. Education inflation is growing at double digit inflation. Medical inflation is even higher. Certain facilities are available at high-end hospitals that are not available to the common person. Recently I met a doctor who works in the cancer department of the Government hospital. She said that the patients who were diagnosed with cancer were not able to continue with the hospital expenses due to the higher medicine costs for cancer. Therefore, it is not just the expenses alone but also a necessity to focus on savings without any choice. Ideally, an unmarried person should save around

30 percent considering his situation. If you are married, your savings should be a minimum of 20–25 percent. Anything lesser than that needs to be addressed immediately.

Chit funds

Chit funds existed in different formats, and the people who need money at any point of time can get benefits with this arrangement. A set of **X** number of people, join and form a chit group for a particular value **Y**. Every month one member from this group requests for some money for his emergency at a discount. This discount is shared by all members and the remaining amount needs to be paid. This discount differs per month. If at any point of time, if any one member fails to pay the amount it creates a problem in the group. So many frauds have happened across India with regard to chit funds. Government regulations were formed but still there is an unorganized market that controls the majority portion.

Sharadha chit fund scam is one of the biggest scams that happened in Kolkata. It is more suitable for people who indulge in business so that they get liquid money quickly. The person who is running the chit fund may be genuine, but if the others who participate fail to pay for a couple of months, everything will be lost. Indulge in chit fund only at your own risk.

Save or live on debts

If you don't find ways to save, then it becomes easy to live life on debts.

The needs of every person keep increasing every year. One easy way is to get loans easily and enjoy things immediately. Further, this makes you to work hard, through which you can earn and pay the bills every month. This makes your life easier now, but not forever. You can't work forever. Although the retirement age is sixty, you can extend working in your business.

Will you have the same vigor as you did in your thirties and forties?

If you have a house as an asset, there is an option to reverse mortgage the house. You can do that arrangement with a bank, where your asset will be validated and a fixed amount is given every month for a specific time period. After your death, the concerned banks will sell the house. This is for those who don't have anything else after retirement.

Understanding your family needs

Raj is involved in high-end consumer products. He was running his business for the last four years and he is successful. He had invested most of his money back into his business. Every time he had excess money, he invested it in infrastructure. Suddenly his family asked him to buy land and construct a house instead of paying rent. So he

TAKE YOUR FIRST STEP

got into a tight liquidity situation. He needs to complete his house construction and he had his home loan EMI underway.

He approached me to start investing in mutual funds a year back. After telling him about the need for financial planning, he understood the need for him to consider budgeting. He has not been withdrawing a fixed salary from his business. He has been taking money once in ten days from his business account for himself and his family needs.

First thing he did was to withdraw a fixed amount for his rent, family needs, his needs, etc. Now he knows how much income he needs to generate every month. Now he is on his way to saving a fixed amount every month.

Taking the first step is the most difficult part. One of my friends got into the trap of closing his home loan EMI. At the same time, he had started his business. Therefore, he has been generating profits and closing it down. He was afraid of the EMI and wanted to get it over with at the earliest. Then as suggested he reduced his monthly home loan EMI and started saving the same amount in mutual funds for his child education. He then started saving INR 6000 now. He was happy now that his child's education is secured.

Some saving tips:

- Decide to save something every month
- Have a goal of saving X amount in three or a six-month period

- Inform your life partner or brother or sister or your parents, so that they question you if you are following it regularly
- Open a separate bank account to put this amount
- Pay for this account within the first week of every month
- If you are interested in buying something, wait for the discount days. This can be done until saving, becomes a habit for you.

Summary

1. Difficulty in savings
2. Chit funds
3. Understanding your family needs
4. Some saving tips

Action points

1. How much did you save in the last three months
2. How much did you save in the last six months
3. How much you want to save from this month?
4. Start allocating that amount in second savings account
5. Declare this savings with your wife or father or mother

CHAPTER 4

Securing Your Life

Insurance is a risk management product from a period dating back to 600 BC hailing from Greece and in various forms. Across the world, this was used to reduce the risk. Modern insurance started from the early 17th century in England.

In India, the oldest existing insurance company is National Insurance Company formed in 1906. In 1956, all life insurance companies were amalgamated and formed the Life Insurance Corporation of India. To penetrate into the Indian market, life insurance with returns was promoted so that people start saving for their future. All the general insurance companies were amalgamated and formed four companies in 1973. Privatization opened up the foreign and private entities from 1990.

Insurance should be seen as a product to cover your risks during tough times. In India, the interest rates were higher from 1960 to early 2000s, and thus everyone got the notion that interest rates will always stay in double digits. Endowment policies through Life

Insurance companies gave returns based on these interest rates. Hence, it favored the people. They were safe and reliable.

Once interest rates started reducing from 2000, you can see a big question mark recently,

"Do I really need this policy as an investment?"

Again, due to the unawareness about other products, it led to many people buying any one policy or being sold to you by many of the intermediaries during tax filing season.

Types of Insurance

There are two broad categories of insurance:

1. Life Insurance
2. General Insurance

Life insurance includes term insurance, endowment plans, money back plans etc. They protect your life.

General Insurance consists of health insurance, home insurance, car insurance, two-wheeler insurance, etc. They protect all other things apart from your life.

Why you need Insurance?

To protect yourself from an unforeseen situation. Think about the AMCs you take with consumer durable companies or warranty you would take with cars, bikes, etc. All these protect your durables from bigger damages.

Similarly, in your life, if anything happens to you, there will be an emotional and financial loss. Emotional loss may take time and it will not affect a lot of people apart from your family members and friends. Consider the financial loss—your parents' care, your kid's education—now and in the future are all at stake.

A simple personal accident policy along with health insurance would have made things easier. Consider taking insurance to prevent financial losses.

It is recommended to have these basic insurances even before starting your investment planning,

1. Term Insurance
2. Personal Accident policy
3. Health Insurance
4. Critical Illness policy

Vehicle insurance should be taken by default because without that, you will not be able to drive your vehicles.

Term Insurance

Term Insurance is the life insurance that everyone must possess. It offers a bigger coverage at a lesser premium. When you compare this to endowment plans, the premium will be much higher for bigger coverage. If you have bigger liabilities, you can take this policy under

Marriage Women policy act where the entire proceeds go to the wife in the absence of her husband.

The only disadvantage with the term plan is that you will not be able to get back your paid premium and it needs to be renewed on a yearly basis. Based on your age, this premium may differ but once you take a policy at twenty-five, it will remain the same for the entire policy period. Ideally, you can take the policy of ten to twelve times your salary.

Personal Accident policy
The number of accidents in India is on the rise and even though you are driving carefully, or you don't have vehicles to drive, the chances of meeting with an accident are there. This policy helps you in these situations.

You may get a partial disability, temporary disability, and permanent disability out of this accident. In all the situations, compensation is provided based on the severity of the accident. Some of the companies may even cover the cost of an accident due to burns. Some may even provide compensation to take rest and this is purely based on a case-to-case basis.

Death due to an accident receives monetary compensation only in this cover and not in Health Insurance.

Health Insurance

Medical expenses are on the rise and there is something called medical inflation. This is similar to inflation where there is a rise in the price of common products. To protect you from unforeseen medical situations due to illness, this health insurance helps.

Major advantage is if you are under cover, you can opt for a cashless claim. Your health insurance company will pay all your bills to the hospital and generally 5–10 percent of the bills have to be borne by us.

Only thing you should have in mind is that, you need to take a health insurance when you are healthy. There is high chance of your policy being rejected once you get any disease like diabetes, asthma, hypertension, etc.

Critical Illness policy

This policy ensures that you get a one-time settlement immediately once the doctor diagnoses and provides a report. Unlike the health insurance policy, which requires your entire report along with the discharge summary, the claim toward this policy is simple.

You need to look at the list of major illnesses covered by this policy before buying it and applying for a claim. Heart-related ailments, lungs, liver ailments, etc. would be covered under this critical illness policy. Cancer is not covered after a certain stage and it differs with different insurance companies.

Once you get a huge settlement, this can allow you to take a little more rest from your business or office routine.

Returns from Insurance

"Insurance is not an investment;" if someone is selling an insurance policy as an investment please tell this to them. As per IRDA rules, the standard returns which insurance companies need to give is just 4 percent and 8 percent, but in many tier 1 and tier 2 cities, this is being mis-sold as high return policies.

Mainly you may be forced to buy a child insurance policy, first of all this is issued based on your data and your child will be included in that policy. Incase anything happens to you, the sum assured will be given toward your child's education needs. If you have high sum assured Term Insurance plan, will this child insurance policy be needed?

The best way to calculate the needed insurances for anyone is to first list down the following:

1. Money required for your child's higher education
2. Money required for your home in your absence
3. Home loan\car loan\personal loan

Now you know the total liabilities and the money requirement in the future. Then look at your salary structure or your yearly tax returns.

If your yearly income is X, then you are eligible for ten to twelve times your yearly income (12x).

On top of all this, as this is a pure term plan, you can take the policy online from most companies at a lesser premium.

Cost of insurance

One of the drawbacks pointed out was, if I am not using this insurance for the rest of my life, it will be a waste of premium made for term, health, critical illness, and personal accident policies.

Let us look at the premium made for all these four policies for a thirty-year-old person

Term Insurance (sum assured - 1 crore) – INR10,000
Family Floater Health Insurance (sum assured - 10 lakhs) – INR 12,000

Critical Illness policy (25 lakhs) – INR 8000
Personal Accident policy (25 lakhs) – INR 4000

First advantage is that all these are covered under section 80 C and 80 D. You can straightaway get tax exemptions.

Second advantage is if you are paying INR 35,000 as risk premium for your life if anything happens to you, your family life will be secured financially. If any health issues arise in your family, they will be protected with Health Insurance and critical illness. Any accidents are covered under personal accident policy.

Third advantage is, after fifteen years of having this policy along with a steady investment planning going on, if any serious health issue happens, won't you look at saving your life instead of protecting your wealth?

Fourth advantage is that there may be unforeseen situations where we may not have emergency money. These policies help in taking care of our life in all aspects.

These will protect your health and wealth in a way.

Term Insurance - case study

An incident happened a few years back, where one of the clients who has been paying premium for years with a leading insurance company suddenly died and he had a debt of 10 lakhs.

After few weeks, the Insurance officials went with a check of 2 lakhs because his sum assured was two lakhs only. Their family asked the officials just one question, "Why wasn't the sum assured higher?"

For the premium he had paid, he could have received the best term insurance plan, but he had bought an endowment plan. There may be so many reasons for his decision, but from now on, make sure you are buying an insurance based on the calculation mentioned above.

Health Insurance - case study

Ragavi had recently increased her health insurance premium to 20 lakhs on renewal. She was perfectly all right. She had maintained insurance and investments separately. By now, their family accumulated substantial wealth for their kid's education abroad.

After a few months, all of a sudden, she had developed lumps on her body. On diagnosis, it was confirmed as cancer. It was in stage 1 and it was treatable. The cost didn't matter as it was getting covered under the health insurance policy. She is completely cured of cancer now.

Traditional plans:

Money back policy, **Endowment plans,** etc. may not be suitable if you are in your thirties. People in the late forties or fifties can take this policy in order to meet their retirement corpus. These policies can almost provide guaranteed returns.

Annuity plans are a must if you have subscribed for National Pension System (NPS). There are different kinds of annuity plans. This is again a safe product for retired people to park their accumulated corpus. They can get a fixed monthly amount.

How to avoid mis-selling

Most of the insurance products are mis-sold during the period of January to March. This is the time each one of you rushes to invest under section 80C and complete the tax formalities. It is easy for people to sell during this period, as each one of you ask for safety and guaranteed returns.

As per IRDA norms, all insurance products can be sold with returns at 4 percent and 8 percent only. When someone is selling you endowment plans, they will show this projection only. In case of ULIP, they will show you the past returns. When the stock market is doing good, it is easy for them sell ULIP as the returns will always be higher. As the "premium paying term" is only five years, you would have been sold stating this is a five-year policy. ULIP will generate good returns only if you keep paying it for more than ten years. It is a long-term investment product. The insurance cover will not be enough.

Enquire about the below points, before buying any insurance:

1. Get to know fully about the product
2. Be clear if it is ULIP or Endowment or Money back plan
3. Make sure you know the full premium paying term
4. Take time to analyze your situation and the need for such a policy
5. Ask an expert, if you still have doubts

Summary

1. Insurance is not an investment.
2. Have four basic insurances to protect your life and dependents.
3. Gain knowledge before choosing any policy.
4. How to avoid mis-selling?

Action points

Consider having these insurance policies at the earliest:

1. Term Insurance
2. Health Insurance
3. Critical Illness policy
4. Personal Accident policy

CHAPTER 5

Tomorrow's Essential

How many of you know grasshopper and ant story? There lived a grasshopper and an ant, who were neighbors. During the summer, the grasshopper played all day along. Enjoying the summer, he didn't think about the immediate winter. The ant on the other hand had been working tirelessly in accumulating food for the winter season. Winter arrived and things started changing. The grasshopper couldn't get enough food as he couldn't go out and he stayed in his house. The ant that had accumulated all the necessary food in his place was happily eating.

This story is not about friendship, so there was no possibility of the ant sharing his food with the grasshopper. It is about saving for your future. The ant has invested its time and accumulated food during the summer. It started reaping the benefits of eating food during the difficult winter period.

Now, how many of you save and invest when you are earning?

Further, investing is essential on the backdrop of inflation. If you are having any cash left over in a bank account, it can give you some interest. This is called savings. When this amount is invested as fixed deposit or recurring deposit, it is called an investment.

Value investing

Value Investing gained its place when Warren Buffet started using it while purchasing stocks. Buying a stock at its *intrinsic value* and selling it on a high. When you sit and think about it, this is what you will do while purchasing any piece of land or apartment. If it is gold, we will calculate a lot like whether it will increase in the immediate future.

The common form of value investing that we do in India is in real estate. Whenever you are going to purchase a flat, your promoter will load it with values that he is offering which is nothing but value for money or value investing. Look into buying something when it is beaten down.

Gold can be bought when it is beaten down. It is the best hedging investment product. Though from 2011 the price didn't increase the average value it generated over the period of last 20 years stays at around 9 percent.

Real estate can be considered when there is no activity is happening, as most of the unsold inventories will then be available at lesser value.

In the stock market, you can take a contra approach. Take any time period, where a few of the sectors will do extremely well and there is a sector that will not be looked into. Find those sectors and in that find a stock to invest in for a longer period of time.

All the above points can be done only if you are clear. Else, it is best advised to approach a financial advisor.

The reason to approach a financial advisor is to understand your risk tolerance and risk capacity.

If you are young, you can invest in equities and you can tolerate a loss to the maximum of X percent. When you are sixty, you will not be able to have the same level of tolerance for losses. This varies with individuals and with ages as well. There cannot be a simple yardstick to measure the risk tolerance of every individual.

Risk capacity, you may be young, but you might have dependents and other emergencies to take care of. In this scenario, you should not invest in equities as this can be called risk capacity. A person at sixty may have a higher risk capacity if he received a regular pension and was left with a bigger sum for investment.

It takes lot of effort to understand these two things and invest accordingly. You may be biased while finding your attributes and hence the need for an expert who can advise correctly. It can be your parents, friends, family members, etc. but it should be without prejudice.

Investment mindset

An investment mindset is the most needed one in relation to money, knowledge, job, business, or anything. People who fear a lot tend to lose a lot. You can win only when you have the focus and belief in it. When you fear for something then you tend to lose your focus.

Investments can be anything, let us take the case of real estate as the most preferred way of investing. When you don't believe in your investment then you will buy a plot in a place where there is no resale value. When you are in need of money urgently, then you will tend to lose money by selling at half the price.

One of my clients had an interest for buying real estate plots or building homes for rentals. He had two homes for rental income in a tier 2 city. He also bought a home in a tier 1 city, for living along with rental income. He started getting problems from the people who were renting his house. Then he had developed a notion that rentals were not his cup of tea and that he will face problems with them. Due to this notion, he got problems from people in tier 2 rental homes as well.

You should believe in something for it to happen and don't let the fear come in your way.

Why equity is essential?

Warren Buffet and equity are two sides of the same coin according to me. When you start talking about the stock market the topic automatically shifts toward the lessons of Warren Buffet. He had started investing from the age of eleven and he had cursed himself for not starting earlier.

He accumulated more than 90 percent of his assets after he turned forty-nine. Across the world, all the wealth managers will have only a proportion in equities when it comes to asset management. When it comes to Buffet, he advises 100 percent investment into equities and he has the evidence to support his argument.

Equity is one of the most volatile investment products if you look at the short-term perspective. If you look at the long term, it can create wealth like no other asset.

Take the classic case of Wipro and Infosys, the darlings of the Indian IT Industries. In the 1980s and 1990s no one anticipated the IT revolution or the IT industry domination. Investing in these companies would have been like investing in barren lands. If you had invested INR 1000 in Wipro shares in 1981, your net worth would be more than 56 crores by now. If you had invested INR 9500 during 1991 in Infosys shares, it would have been worth 5 crores now.

Both INR 1000 and INR 9500 would have been a bigger amount during those time periods. When it comes to investing, all it takes is small amount of savings over a period of time and investing in something like this, which is worth it.

SME IPO

SME IPO gained its importance because of the returns it generated in the last few years. Some of the prominent investors like Rakesh Jhunjhunwala, Porinju Veliyath etc. have also invested in this platform.

SME IPO is run by the stock exchange. SEBI doesn't control this. Small and medium enterprises who want to expand come to this platform to generate the required money from the public. The minimum investment amount is 1 lakh so then only people with known risks about the company invest in this platform.

Why equity may not be for you?

Though equity creates assets, it is also the mass destroyer of wealth. Equity investments may not be for you:

1. If you are a first time investor
2. If you are investing all your investments into this asset
3. If you are investing based on someone else's tips
4. If you have the slightest doubts
5. If you are not clear while buying a stock
6. If you are investing your emergency fund
7. If you are not follower of the stock market

There can be many other reasons and these can be the top things, you should have in mind if you are going to invest in the stock market.

There are classic examples in everyone else's life, your dad, mom, friend, or family member would have lost an enormous amount of money in the stock market.

In India, during 2008, infrastructure was the booming sector with a big potential for growth. Those who had invested in some of the top companies like GMR and Suzlon had lost enormous wealth. These companies have not yet recovered, even in 2018.

Why could mutual funds be for you?

Mutual funds are one product where you have many combinations available. Mutual funds are not only about the stock market. It has debt funds which invest in government bonds, commercial papers, etc. Based upon the timeline that you are going to stay invested, you can choose debt, equity, hybrid, or ETFs.

You can choose a fund based on the days to any number of years that you are going to stay invested. Risk factors increase gradually from the days to years. If you are investing for just a day, it can be liquid funds. If you want it in a year, it can be a short-term fund and if you want to invest for more than five years, you can invest in equity mutual funds.

Why you need to stick to the above formula is because of the associated risk. Equity mutual funds are for more than three or four years of investment and if you wish to withdraw by the end of the first or second year, it may be negative. This makes it clear before investing, and you can stay invested until the timeline is achieved.

Equity mutual funds invest in an array of thirty to forty stocks and across sectors. Even if a couple of sectors fail to perform, the returns will not come down drastically, as in the case of direct equities.

Mutual funds can aid you in creating wealth irrespective of your income, and it is one of the better options over any other funds. One of the options available with mutual funds is it can be invested on a monthly basis in the name of SIP or Systematic Investment Planning.

For some of the goals like kid's education or retirement, which is surely long term, you can start investing via SIP. Consider the Reliance Growth fund, which was started with NAV of 10 and now its NAV is 1010 as of 4 October, 2018.

If you had considered investing one lakh in 1996, by now your worth would be 1 crore.

Consider having invested INR 5000 from January 1999 until October 2018. Your invested amount is 11.85 lakhs and your investment value is 1.65 crores.

The above stated examples are illustrations, which you can find everywhere. Please look at the power of compounding in the long run. If you don't have a large sum, you can invest with a monthly investment amount.

Alternate investments

The first time I heard about alternate investments I was thinking, "Can this be an investment product?" Some of the alternate investments available in the market are:

1. Art
2. Wine
3. Diamond index
4. Private equity
5. Investing in startups and companies
6. Other collectibles
7. Hedge funds

All these can give you humongous returns. You also need bigger investment amounts to get into it. Risks associated with the above investments are also huge. You may need to wait for a longer tenure to book profit and at times you might end up at loss.

Art in the short term may not fetch good returns, as it may take a longer tenure for it to fetch good returns. Wine may take decades to fetch good returns. There are some wines, which are as old as a century. Diamonds are another form of investments similar to gold. Private equity and investing in startups are all high-risk investment opportunities. Uber, Facebook, Google, Ola, Flipkart, etc. were startups and those who had invested in this initially had made huge profits.

Bitcoin

Bitcoin came into the limelight last year and has been in the investor radar for quite a while. People who never participated in equities showed interest in owning a bitcoin. By the end of December 2017, its value was touching $20,000 and by January, it gradually started falling. It was banned in India and in many more countries. Only few countries didn't clear the rules against it. In India, many who had invested in bitcoin lost a huge sum of money.

By December 2018, the value of one bitcoin is less than $5000. An investor who had invested in bitcoin at its peak by now would have lost everything.

Things to learn:

1. Never invest in unknown products
2. Look for a clear instruction from RBI or SEBI in India
3. Never invest based on third party advertisements

Will writing and its importance

You may remember the importance of will writing in old Indian movies. First generation rich people will write a will or may forget to write one. Second generation people will fight for the assets over a period. This can turn into enmity among relationships.

Will writing is not only for rich people. Anyone can leave behind his or her legacy using a will. You may have an endowment plan, mutual funds, shares, real estate, commerce properties, jewelry etc. All these can be clearly mentioned as to whom you want to give it to. You need to do this in front of witnesses when you are in a clear state of mind.

Summary

1. Value investing and its importance
2. Investment mindset
3. Why equity is essential
4. Why equity may not be for you
5. Why mutual funds may be for you
6. Alternate investments
7. Will writing and its importance

Action points

1. How much are you investing for your future goals?
2. How much are you investing in equities?
3. How much are you investing in other asset classes?
4. Do you invest based on your time period?

CHAPTER 6

Various Ways

"Don't put all your eggs in one basket."

Many in the financial services industry quote this. If someone invests only in one of the assets like equity, it will be quoted to him to diversify his investments. Investments started from the time people started exchanging products and slowly the income of people who had traded a lot started increasing. They had started purchasing more gold. The world has evolved over the years but if you look at the investment returns and patterns, it has remained mostly the same. The best example to elucidate this is Warren Buffet when it comes to equity and value investing. Robert Kiyosaki of *Rich Dad, Poor dad* believes in real estate investment.

In India, the known investment types are real estate and gold. Equity as an investment is slowly getting its reach.

Broadly, there can be two types of assets:
1. Physical assets
2. Financial assets

Physical assets are the ones that you can see, touch, and feel. Gold and real estate are the best examples of physical assets. Many would like to have physical assets as it gives the sense of ownership. It can be shown off easily and you can be proud about your achievement. Value of the investment can be seen by comparing it in the open market.

Financial assets are not tangible like physical assets, but it will grow virtually and can be redeemed in a bank. All bank deposits, shares, mutual funds, etc. are financial assets.

Let us look at all the available investment products and their features:

1. Gold
2. Real estate
3. Equity or share market
4. Mutual funds
5. Fixed deposits
6. Post office deposits
7. Alternate investments

Gold

The Indian households all together hold more than 20,000 tons of gold. This clearly shows the power and belief in gold as an investment. In the last few decades, gold has grown as an investment product also. Thereafter people started buying gold coins in huge numbers.

In the last twenty years, considering the gold purchased during the *Akshaya Tritiya* period, it has given close to 10 percent returns. [*Source*: ET Wealth]

Real estate

Real estate is one of the best investments. It is a dream to hold a piece of land and have a house built in that place. Real estate can start generating secondary income and you should buy land based on those criteria.

For example, a commercial space can be rented out for high returns as compared to residential rentals. The only major concern has been the liquidity, and you need to hold onto it for longer time period of five to ten years in certain cases for it to grow.

The best example has been the case of McDonalds, which started out as a fast food chain but now holds many land parcels across the world. They lease out their franchise in their place for rent. Their company worth is close to 28 billion mainly due to their real estate returns.

Equity or share market

Equity or share market is one of the most exciting avenues where many fail, while looking at few people making humongous returns. If you have registered a private limited company, you may list your company in the stock exchange as BSE or NSE. Share value may be arrived at based on the company's profit and loss account. Once listed, people start trading on that share on a daily basis.

Right from Macro conditions like crude oil, currency exchange, global uncertainty, trade war, etc., to micro domestic situations like monsoon, political instability, drought, fiscal deficit, inefficient budget, etc., everything can affect a share price. Once in a quarter, company results will be announced, and this along with other factors makes a huge impact on the share price. Some make a profit and some lose it.

In India right from 1979, Sensex had given around 12 percent returns and some specific stocks have made huge fortunes for the buyers.

Mutual funds

If you find it difficult to invest in the share market, mutual funds can be the best option. There are two types of mutual funds, one which invests in the stock market and the other one is called debt funds, which doesn't invest in the stock market.

There are other types like hybrid funds, which is a combination of both. Let us look at equity mutual funds where, in the long term it gives more than 15 percent as compounded returns. Benchmark returns are 12 percent.

In case of debt funds, there are products like liquid funds, which can be invested for a day to GILT for long duration funds, which can be invested for more than five years.

There are products for all situations and for everyone in mutual funds.

Fixed deposits

Fixed deposit is a traditional investment and you can claim tax deduction if you are putting your money in a five-year tax saving deposit.

Post office deposits

Post offices are present in most of the zip codes in India and it has created trust among the public. Post office PPF, fixed deposit, senior citizen savings scheme, etc. are considered safe and many hold their deposits.

Alternate investments

Alternate investments include investments made in wine, diamond, art, etc. There is pride in owning things. Unless you have an interest in any of the above, it is difficult to buy and hold onto for a longer period.

ULIP

ULIP in the current version is an investment product, based on the current expense ratio but the return needs to be validated, over the next few years. One thing to hold in mind is that you need to pay for the entire period, to have a better double digit return from ULIP. You should look at ULIP as an investment product for the entire fifteen- to twenty-year period.

Again, this can be part of your plan but this will not suffice for any one goal completely.

Asset diversification

Every asset has a risk involved in it. Gold will not perform when equities are performing. Returns from gold as an investment is lesser than 5 percent in the last seven to eight years. Real estate may not give humongous returns in the short term and the risk of someone else taking it up will come through.

Equity may give big returns but there is a huge volatility over a period of time. Traditional deposits don't generate a lot of returns to beat inflation itself.

You need to look after lifestyle expenses as well. One solution is diversifying your assets. Gold as an asset can be around 10 percent of your portfolio. Equity portion is based on the age and risk taking capabilities. Real estate can be around 30–40 percent based on the rentals it is yielding.

Let us look at an example of the portfolio of a forty-year-old person. This will vary from person to person:

Look at your age and start analyzing your portfolio now.

Gold	10 percent
Real estate	30–50 percent
Equity	40–50 percent
Deposits	5 percent
Emergency fund	5 percent

Asset diversification reduces the concentrated risk in one asset class alone. If you are clear on how each investment works, it is best to diversify the investment in different assets.

Rule of 72

One thing you should definitely know while investing is the Rule of 72.

Any investment product has a period of investment and returns as percent. If you know any one of these two, you can invest based on whether this product will be able to double your returns.

1) Consider Mutual funds with Benchmark returns of 12:
72 / 12 = 6
Your amount will get doubled in six years.

If you look at the history of equity mutual fund returns of long-term funds, it has been more than 18 percent. Then there is a chance of the amount getting doubled in less than four years.

2) Consider insurance returns, which gets doubled in twenty years (this is how it is sold),
Yes, you can divide 72 by the number of years to find the exact returns that the product is offering:
72 / 20 = 3.6 or approximately 4 percent

Endowment plans can approximately fetch these returns in twenty long years.

The biggest advantage of this rule is that if anyone says your amount will get doubled in X years, you can directly question them on their validity. Most of the Ponzi schemes lure investors with their promos that offer a huge return in quick time.

Ponzi schemes

It's not about literacy when it comes to identifying Ponzi schemes. It is all about the common basics that can help you in identifying it. Even an Indian cricketer from Bangalore had fallen prey to some Ponzi schemes in Bangalore. He had lost nearly four crores. The company had promised about 40 percent returns.

These can be identified once we apply these common basics:

Promise of higher returns - if someone offers higher returns on their products by comparing it with existing products. This should be the first alarm for you.

Complex investment plans - they will not explain the intricacies of how the company is making such huge profits. Transparency is the second alarm for you.

Business models - in this model you would have invested and lost. It is a pyramid model, you need to bring in two people and they in turn need to bring in two more people. Mainly those who joined are paid by the later people. Those who come last will not get anything.

Validity of the company - financial services companies should have been registered with the Ministry of Company Affairs or registered with the SEBI for carrying out related services.

Recently, Yuvraj Singh's mother has invested close to one crore based on the promise of huge returns. She was able to retrieve only fifty lakhs. This news came in the leading news daily.

Why should Fixed Deposit be least preferred?

We had seen a lot about the relationship between inflation and its returns.

For example, in the current scenario, it is offering 7 percent, and India prefers to control the inflation going forward. This will further bring down the interest rates. Then the time period required to double your money will increase more.

For example, a 1 lakh investment at 7 percent returns can take up to ten years in the current scenario as per rule of 72.

If the interest rates are further reduced automatically, the number of years taken to double the investment will become a bit longer. You need to pay the taxes for the interest earned, based on the tax slab you fall under. You are going to earn INR 7000 for an investment of 1 lakh. If you are falling under the 30 percent tax bracket, on INR 7000, 30 percent will be deducted as tax.

Now, consider the inflation and the other expenses for you are around 7 percent. At this rate, your expenses will also double in the next ten years. If an investment doubles on par with inflation, you need to look at other options seriously.

Liquidity - case study

In life, you need liquidity at important times as you may not know when you will need money urgently. Remember that this amount may be higher than the emergency fund that you have by now.

Financial assets help you with this liquidity easily. Recently, I have been discussing with a client to plan for his life separately and not based on how much he is earning for the last two years. He is one of the most successful businessmen in the last twenty-five years.

Last year he had put his son in an engineering college in Bangalore. Now his son wants to join a college in Hong Kong and he couldn't deny this big opportunity for his son. This new college cost 10 lakhs upfront and the same amount for next three years. He didn't expect this huge fees requirement. Until now he had made all his money through real estate and whenever he had a surplus he would invest in that. He couldn't liquidate any of those real estate investments.

In this situation, he closed his insurance policy, which fetched him close to 8 lakhs. After calculating based on Rule of 72, the returns were only close to 8 percent. Once he calculated the amount, he was in shock.

The point here is that real estate doesn't offer liquidity when we are in need, and unknown products based on someone else's advice may fetch you poor returns.

Summary

1. Two broad asset types: physical and financial
2. Various investment products are available to choose from
3. Asset Diversification – an important tool to minimize the risk arising from any one investment
4. Rule of 72 – to identify the time taken by your investment to become double
5. Protection from Ponzi schemes
6. Liquidity should be a priority

Action points

1. Assess your current assets as Physical and Financial
2. Start analyzing your portfolio
3. Look at increasing your financial assets for better liquidity
4. Apply "Rule of 72" while calculating returns of an investment product

CHAPTER 7

How to Choose?

"Conceive, Believe, Achieve."
- Napoleon Hill

The above quote is one of my favourite. It clearly demonstrates how you can achieve something. First, you should conceive the idea then you should have complete conviction about that idea and finally plan the steps to achieve that idea. Napoleon Hill is one of the best self-help authors and is known for his famous book *Think and Grow Rich*, it is still one of the bestselling books although the author died in 1970.

When it comes to investment, you need to conceive the idea that you can be rich and wealthy and then you need to believe in that idea and then finally you can achieve that idea.

Now in real life, you need to know your requirements or your financial goals in life. Then the products and other things can help in the financial goals.

Steve Jobs, Bill Gates, etc. have achieved success from nothing by having a strong conviction about what they are doing. For a few, owning Mercedes Benz is their dream and recently a farmer from Tamil Nadu has done it at the age of eighty-eight, and this was highlighted all over social media.

Hence, if you strongly desire wealth that drives you to earn more, save more and achieve all your aspirations in your life.

Finding your *why*?

Generally, you will choose a product based on the tax saving need or based on how much surplus you have at the end of every month, and this doesn't help you in increasing your savings or any further investments. Ultimately, the thing you need to do is list down your goals or requirements in life, and you can have a big list based on the number of things you want.

If you look at the investment products, not all are long term or short term. Therefore, you need to understand your requirements first.

You will work with a goal for your business without which you will not move an inch in your business.

HOW TO CHOOSE?

Similarly, you need to identify all your requirements or set your targets in your life both for this moment and also for next couple of decades down the line.

You can buy certain things just because you had liked it in your friend's home, you would have bought a car based on a need for your business, the list becomes endless unless you know the high priority requirements in your life.

Remember that you are unique and that your requirements are unique, you just need to sit with your partner and list the requirements as a priority.

Then you need to segregate the list as below:

- Short-term goals can be for a period of few months up to two years;
- Mid-term goals can be for a period of two to five years;
- Long-term goals can be for goals that are beyond five years.

Let us look with examples at each of these categories:

Any emergency needs or things that are going to happen in the next two years can be segregated as short term. You need to take care of your capital and you shouldn't think about making high returns. You need to look at the safety of the capital as a priority in this category.

Midterm goals can be like opting for a house based on your increase in income. You can look to change your car after a few years. Even capital requirement for your business in the next two years is a midterm goal. Anything between two and five years can be classified as midterm. For these kinds of goals you need to look at some better returns than fixed deposit and also look at capital safety.

Long-term goals can be anything beyond five years. Your retirement, home loan closure, buying a second home, kid's education etc. all require a big capital and you can invest in riskier investment products knowing the risks involved in it.

The biggest advantage of doing this is that you will come to know when you need your money. This in turn helps you in choosing the best suitable product for that requirement and goal.

Let us consider a person who is waiting to pay for his son's college education in next twelvemonths and he is falling short of 30 percent of his education fund. He should not invest in the stock market based on the belief provided by someone that he can make a 30 percent return within one year. According to the requirement segregation, this falls under a short-term goal, and he should not invest in this product (which is not suitable for a one-year period).

How to choose an investment product?

Now comes the interesting part of choosing the investment product, at this stage you are clear with the requirements. Once you interact with your parents and friends, you will end up with many interesting stories about how to make money as well as stories about losing everything within a day.

The below criteria can help you in choosing the best suitable product:

- Knowledge
- Age
- Returns
- Years
- Risk

Knowledge

No one has the knowledge about investment products in detail unless you start investing in it. The alarming thing is when you invest in something without knowing the details of it. Please do understand that it is your money and you should allocate some time to try to understand the positives and the negatives before investing.

At least understand where your money is going to be invested, what are the risks involved, when to take the money out, etc. Best thing you can do is to ask these questions and your other doubts before investing. Write down all the details on paper in front of them, by this way you can be clear on what you are doing.

Age

Age should be one of the factors you consider while you are investing in equities. When you are young and just starting your career, the risk taking capabilities can be higher and you can invest in equities.

As your age increases, you can start reducing the equity exposure based on your level of comfort.

The general rule of thumb is (100 - age) is calculated for investment in equities. So once your age increases, the level of equity can be reduced. This is considered as an ideal way to understand how much you can invest in equities.

Returns

Returns are important because fraud happens when people chase returns. Every now and then, there are Ponzi schemes, which show attractive returns with a sustainable growth model for their companies. Ordinary people are the ones who are duped because they need good returns with a lesser investment.

Rule 72 as mentioned in the previous chapter helps you in identifying whether this product is suitable or not.

Years

Years means the number of years that you can stay invested in without taking that money out. This is another important criterion because you know that this money is for a long-term investment and you won't break it.

If you are someone who doesn't have the habit of withdrawing your personal income separately from your business, then you need to follow these criteria diligently. If you're investing for a specific goal, then you shouldn't withdraw that amount for any other purpose.

Risk

Risk is something that is often misunderstood by many. Risk is involved in every aspect of life. From the moment, you close your eyes until the moment you open your eyes, there is no guarantee that you will be alive.

If you are someone who drives a car or bike, you know the risk involved. If you are running a business, you know the risks involved. In the two examples mentioned, you know the risk and how to mitigate the risks to a certain level.

Similarly, even in investments there are risks involved, and it varies with every individual. You may take a risk lightly and the other person may perceive it as complete danger in his life. Therefore, if someone says there is a huge risk involved in any investment, that risk may be much lesser for you.

You are halfway through identifying your goals and inspecting the criteria for choosing the right product. From this stage, you should have the belief on the investment that you have made. The only thing you can do now is monitor it regularly over a time period.

Now you will get the question, "What if the investment I have made doesn't give me good returns?"

Obviously, your investments may not do too well at all times and you should take a hard decision of closing it down and investing it in a better product. There may be instances of a wrong real estate investment, and after enquiring, you know for certain that it will not move for the next few years. Based on your situation you need to decide whether to sell it or invest in other products.

We have discussed various investment products in the previous chapter, so you can refer to that and link it with your goals.

Planning for each stage of life

Until now, you have seen how to conceive your wealth, plan appropriately and believe in your products and eventually achieve it as per the plan. You may decide to take a higher risk when you are in your twenties and you may decide to take a lesser risk when you are in your sixties. Therefore, it is very critical for you to know "Why you need to plan for each stage of life?"

This is essential, as this will determine the level of wealth you are going to accumulate in your life. There is always a difference between doing it now and later. With certain products, you need to wait for a much longer time as it compounds slowly.

In your twenties

The first stage of life is where you will get the taste of earning money, either as an employee or when you start your career with some business. Either way if you are a success, you will end up splurging your money unless you have some responsibilities at home. If you are someone who is very responsible, just look at your friends who you feel might have much more money. They whine about not having anything left, after couple of years.

As this sets the tone of your life, it is highly recommended to save on a regular basis. In my life, my dad asked me about my salary after six months as I was not saving anything in his perspective. I understood his point and from then I started saving a small portion.

How much should I save?

This will be based on the salary, the place you are living in, along with the dependents in your family. Ideal savings should be around 30 percent and considering other factors mentioned start saving and investing at least 10 percent of your salary.

If you are in your twenties it's highly recommended that you invest in equities but again based on your understanding about the product.

In your thirties

In the most important stage of your life, you will be loaded with responsibilities. By now, you would have been married or are going to get married. You may be having kids, thus all your savings and invested amounts would have dwindled down by now largely. You would have reached a critical position in your business and all this may cause a sudden pause.

You should consider topping up your existing Term Insurance as your dependents have increased and plan for additional investments.

The investment amount needs to be increased for additional goals in your life.

Equity portions can be increased or decreased based on your dependency in your family. You should have a family floater health insurance covering your family, along with a personal accident policy and a critical illness policy.

In your forties

Now this is the stage when your business may prosper to next stage, your kids may enter college and you will need to fund them. If you have planned properly for your kid's education when you are in your 30s this becomes a cake walk for you.

By now, you can start increasing your equity portion as your business income might have started increasing. Once you reach late forties you can start reducing the equity allocation in your portfolio.

In your fifties

By now, most of your responsibilities in your family would have got over, and you may start looking at retiring if you have worked hard or are looking at expanding your business. It is your choice.

Start analyzing your retirement portfolio from now on and see if it will be sufficient for you to live on with your corpus from the day you stop going to work. This is the last part of the accumulation stage for many and distribution stage for few.

Accumulation stage means you start accumulating assets in your life, and the distribution stage is where you start utilizing the accumulated assets.

In your sixties

This is an ideal stage for retirement from your business, as per the common person's perception. You can consider retirement if you are financially free and you don't need to worry about funds for the next twenty-five years of your life.

If you are passionate about your business, then you can continue to work for the passion. By now, you should have amassed the retirement corpus as per your lifestyle.

Retirement life and thereafter

This is for people who consider retiring by sixty and start enjoying their life. Many rich people have considered philanthropy after a stage of life. Bill Gates started that and now recently Jack Ma of Alibaba has announced an early retirement. Although they retired, they hold a portion in their companies and that makes them do charity and maintain their lifestyle.

If you are considering retirement or have retired, invest a portion in balanced fund or long-term debt fund and start doing withdrawal through Systematic Withdrawal plan. This way your retirement fund can stay long.

Now wherever you are, you know what is going to happen in each stage of your life. These are family responsibilities and in addition to this, you need to plan for lifestyle expenses, family vacations, a car, smart phones, etc.

Once you understand in which stage of life, you are in and start planning for your goals, finding the right product becomes very easy. It is best advised to have a brief understanding on all products in your twenties so that choosing becomes easy in all other stages of life. There may be a brief change in the way a product works, but the concept of how it works will not change much.

Identify your requirements of life or your financial goal

....
....
....

Choose the investment product based on the criteria

....
....
....

Invest based on which stage of life you are in now

Financial goals differ in each stage of life and that is going to be the base for you to start working on. Then comes the understanding of the products and staying invested in each of the goals. Each stage of life helps you in increasing or reducing the equities and other products in your portfolio.

How much is enough?

I am investing X amount in mutual funds, is that enough?

People start comparing it with their neighbors or friends and think that they are investing a large sum. After forty, you should have increased your income and at that point investing INR 25,000 is not a big deal, right?

Is this enough?

You should seriously ask this to yourself every year.

Consider INR 50,000 as a monthly expense, including monthly groceries, bills, school fees, etc.

Inflation – 8 percent (your expense increases every year at this rate)

By the same Rule of 72, your expenses will double in nine years.

You should safely assume it would take seven or eight years.

Now consider the corpus you have accumulated till now. Average living age is sixty-seven in India and there is a chance for you live until seventy-five.

For example, assuming that from the age of sixty your expense is 1 lakh, calculate how much you should accumulate:

Your corpus should be there until your last breath to enjoy your last retirement age in peace.

It is better to check with an expert if your current investments are enough to manage your retirement life.

Summary

1. Finding your why?
2. How to choose an investment product?
3. Planning for each stage of life
4. How much is enough?

Action points

1. List down your goals
2. If you had invested, understand the product now
3. Check if the investment is sufficed for your goals and for your age.

CHAPTER 8

Outstanding Life

Loans have become an integral part of life. It need not be loans or mortgage alone. If you are having a credit card, then you agreed to make the payment within the next forty to fifty days depending on the credit card company guidelines. Remember, the highest interest rates among all loan products are only with the credit card.

Life has changed drastically in the last few decades. Consumerism has taken the entire world by storm. Everyone wants to have everything and this changed the attitude toward money. If you want to enjoy or have anything in this world, money should not be the problem. You can get a loan to satisfy your needs. There has been a period where one needs to wait his entire life to have his dream house or a dream car.

Now in this modern era, if you want to have a car you can get it on loan, if you want home, you can take a loan. Let us look at different kinds of loans available for a consumer:

- Car loan
- Personal loan
- Home loan
- Mortgage loan
- Education loan
- Credit card

These are the major types and based on the credit score of an individual there are different kinds of loans being offered now. Sometimes loans can help in creating assets. Take the case of home loan, where you are creating an asset in the long run. In the case of mortgage loan, you would have got loan for running your business, for your marriage, or for funding your retirement.

Loans sometimes help in creating assets as mentioned above and also for achieving greater success. We are focusing only on the loans for retailers, which revolve around your personal finance.

Generally, it is advised to not have more than 30–40 percent of your income as loans. This percentage is subjective to your family, dependents, and other factors in your life. All these factors affect the repayment capacity of an individual. Sometimes loans can be rejected if you have already utilized the maximum eligibility criteria and also if one of your checks bounced. A check bounce affects your credibility.

Home loan

One of the biggest achievements in India is to have your home built before you die. After the boom of the IT industry in the last decade, dream of owning the home has become real for many of them. Higher income in the start of the career has forced many to think about buying a house at a younger age. Some of them even went beyond by investing in their second home, which can generate rental yields. Most of these people are first time homebuyers and are not backed by any monetary support. They were dependent on the home loans provided by many of the institutions.

A home loan is provided based on certain criteria. You should have filed your income tax continuously for the last two years. Your loan repaying capacity is an important consideration. If the bank had given you a 1 crore loan without checking your repaying capacity then it will be a big loss for them.

For example, if your income per month is INR 80,000 then banks can offer a home loan of 40 lakhs. This is 50 percent of your monthly income and thus it can be offered as a loan. This can be offered only if you don't have any other loans running in your name.

It is advised not to have more than 35–40 percent of your income as a home loan EMI. You need to consider other important expenses in your life before committing half of your income to a home loan. There have been many instances where people were not able to repay the loan, and their house went up for auction.

Ravi was running a plastic manufacturing company and his company was running in profit. Therefore, he along with his wife took a loan for building their dream home. They exceeded 50 percent of their average monthly income. They took the risk, as production in business was expected to go up as orders were about to come in the next two months. All of a sudden, that project was shut down and their income dipped a bit. It reflected in their monthly expenditures as well. They were cutting short their monthly expenses as much as possible. Finally, they gave up their dream home, as they knew that they were in a dire situation where they could save either their home or their company. They took a decision to save their company and gave up their home loan immediately. The only thing that favored them was that someone was there to buy their home. Points to note before taking a home loan:

1. How much monthly amount can be allocated toward paying a home loan?
2. What expenses can be cut short immediately?
3. Risk factors if things don't work out the way you planned
4. Emergency funds for paying home loan EMIs
5. What are the expenses, which will come in the next three years?

All these questions help you in getting a clear picture of whether should you consider a home loan now or if it can be postponed. Just think of buying a home after five years, the price will not surge a lot in your surroundings. There may be a surge in a few areas, but think about the difficulties you will face if you take it now. Instead, you can postpone your buying by a few months or years. Use this time to set your priorities right in your life. These measures will help you in achieving everything in life and also brings in clarity.

Home loan vs. SIP

The most bizarre thing in life is that you will take a loan for twenty years and after three months, you will start planning to close it down in three to five years. The reason is now only you will start to analyze the interest portion of the loan. For a twenty-year loan, in the initial 10 year period you will be paying more of an interest. Principal will get knocked off in big proportion after eleventh year only.

For example, if you are taking a home loan of 50 lakhs now, you will end up paying one crore in twenty years. An extra 50 lakhs is paid as an interest portion. Instead, if you close it in three to five years, you can save a lot of the interest portion.

After this eureka moment, you will end up working hard, to pay the dues on time. Finally, you may end up closing it in five years. Considering that your age was around thirty when you took the loan and then you ended up closing your entire loan in your late thirties. This is the golden period of your life.

One suggestion may be starting a SIP, by opening a mutual fund account at the same time.

If your loan is 35 lakhs, pay up to five lakhs for a period of three to five years and then simultaneously start investing INR 5000 in mutual funds via SIP.

If you have been paying the EMI of INR 30,818 for twenty years, the total amount paid by you is INR 73,96,400.

If you have closed five lakhs in five years, this may effectively come down to 65 lakhs (approximately).

Instead of reducing the tenure, reduce the monthly EMI amount to INR 25,000. The rest of the amount has to be invested in Mutual Funds.

The monthly amount invested in twenty years is 12 lakhs.

Returns at 15 percent - 66 lakhs
Returns at 12 percent - 46 lakhs

Historically equity mutual funds have given more than 15 percent and you can end up receiving 50 lakhs in twenty years.

This way, you can also look at investing for other aspirations. You can also consider a tax deduction for the interest portion that you are paying as an option to save tax. Avoiding paying the interest is the number one reason for people closing their home loan quickly and this section can help you think in an alternate way. It's up to you to consider how to close it.

The biggest irony is that those who closed their home loans ended up buying a second home as an investment in another few years. Therefore, it is worth waiting for few years to buy your real dream home instead of some random home.

Reducing tenor vs. EMI amount
Again, there can be a big debate on which is the best suited option among reducing tenor or EMI amount. No one can guarantee returns on an investment that you are going to make, but you know how much you are going to pay as interest.

Reducing the monthly EMI can give you a small option of investing for other aspirations in life. The stress of a loan will always be there.

Reducing tenor can help in closing the loans faster and the stress is completely reduced, once you pay it out completely.

Buying a second home on loan
Think twice before taking any major financial decisions, the first time it can be attributed to emotional factors. Before buying a home for the second time, think about all the factors that has been highlighted as in the above sections.

If you are buying home purely for bigger space, think about whether you can sell the existing home to buy the new one. This can give you a lot of freedom.

If you are not constrained by money, then you are free to make your choice of investments.

When to opt for a personal loan?

Personal loans are easily available and this is a curse for many. As it is easily available, you end up buying things using a loan. It can be for marriage, immediate emergency needs, etc. You need to look at the consequences of buying a personal loan, as if you are not able to pay, your credit score will come down.

The credit score will come down irrespective of the loans you have taken. Any missing payments may result in you being a defaulter. This will bring down your credit score and you will not be able to get any other loans.

Sometimes you would have paid all the installments and the financing institution would not have updated your record as closed. This may also result in showing your profile as a defaulter. It is better to get the *no objection certificate* once you have paid all the installments and get a free credit score report.

Credit card

One of my clients has given a loan to his friend. He gave a loan and expected that he will get it back in a month's time. He doesn't have any backup, and so he is dependent on his monthly income. After a month, the person who borrowed the amount couldn't repay it and in two months he went to another company. Meanwhile my friend started using his credit card to manage his expenses. From one credit card, he bought another credit card. Credit cards have a credit limit, which made his life easy. In six months, he had accumulated 2 lakhs as his outstanding amount. He realized that interest that he was paying is huge in his statement.

Finally, he decided to pay off the entire amount by taking a personal loan. The personal loan has interest to be paid within the range of 12–14 percent and the credit card has an interest in the range of 35–40 percent. The only solution is to pay off your credit card outstanding every month.

Points to note before taking any loans

1. Be aware of the cash flow in your family
2. Discuss with your partner or dependents
3. Prepare an emergency fund for paying EMIs in case of an emergency
4. Have a plan by when you will be closing your loan
5. Make sure the loan amount does not exceed more than 40 percent of your income
6. Tell yourself not to panic after the EMI has started
7. See the interest chart before signing up for the loan

Summary

1. Types of loans
2. Home loan vs. SIP
3. Reducing tenor vs. EMI amount
4. When you should opt for a personal loan
5. Points to note before taking any loan

Action points

1. List down your loans.
2. Check the number of credit cards you own.
3. See if your loan is creating asset.
4. Close down your loans one by one if it is not adding value.

CHAPTER 9

Life with Style

"Lifestyle is nothing but living your life in style."

Lifestyle is nothing but how you want to live your life. It is easy to understand that with the available money flow you may be forced to live a mean life.

The life of each generation varies. Let us look at the present situation. After liberalization, India slowly moved toward globalization. Everything took time, but people started embracing the change in lifestyle. Right from a refrigerator, washing machine, bike, car, shopping malls, movies, LCD, LED, etc., the things that were once available to only few people, is now available to everyone.

All these changes in your life, makes life so easy. Branding yourself plays an important role. If you are wearing a particular brand, you will be categorized as X. If you are wearing another brand, you will be categorized as Y. People identify you by the way you dress, you travel, you live, etc. these have become lifestyle measures. If you are following a simple life, then you will be categorized as meager person.

If you opt for branded clothing and accessories, it can cost you a lot. It doesn't end there. You need to start maintaining it for all occasions. You need to groom yourself with regard to your clothes and accessories.

All these have grown in the last decade. It is obvious that it is an additional expense for every family in the last decade. Going by the general inflation chart, the price of these goods increase by 8 percent every year. Some of them rise even more than that.

Mean life or meaningful life

It is up to you to decide whether to have a mean or meaningful life. You need to live a mean life, if you are climbing up a ladder in your business or are in your study phase. If you are still living a mean life just because you were brought up in that way during your childhood, you don't need to.

Lifestyle literally means the way a person lives. Currently, there are so many things, which help in improving your standard of living. You can either watch TV on old LCD screen or switch to an LED TV for better clarity only if you can afford it.

One of my friend's parents used to commute via bus although they are leading a comfortable life in Bangalore. Commuting by OLA or Uber would not generate a big hole in their monthly budget. This is the simple lifestyle change that I am referring to.

Ola was started when Bhavish Agarwal, the founder, was finding it difficult to travel in Bangalore. One night he was travelling in a cab, which went in the wrong route and charged him extra. This made him provide cab trips at a much lesser price with extra features.

Ola, Swiggy, etc., have made everything available at our doorstep at the tap of our mobile. Isn't this a luxury?

Luxury

Luxury differs from person to person. Twenty years ago, we had a color TV in Chennai. My brother and I used to visit my grandparents in the rural part of Tamil Nadu. If you are having a TV in that village, then you are a luxurious person. Only two or three households had a TV in that village. During weekends, most of the families will gather around those homes to watch a Sunday movie.

After ten years when I went as a college student, I saw a huge shift. Most of the houses had bikes and the TV had become normal in every household. A shift in luxury happens automatically. It is up to you to go for it at the earliest or wait until your peers force you to get that luxury.

"I am finding it difficult to make ends meet. How can I think about luxury?"

Don't worry, I hear you. You can achieve it only if you come to know about all the available luxuries. Then you can plan about achieving it.

Luxury is associated with authenticity. Consider a watch or leather goods, which are the symbols of luxury for many. All these watches are available for half the rate in their respective local market. Some people will think that non-luxury goods are fake and inferior. One part of the brain will always say that luxurious items are authentic and of superior quality. Hence, luxury items are always associated with self-esteem and hence the strong emotional attachment increases.

Everything matters

If you are on a cruise, you will be enjoying the beauty of the cruise. On the last day of the cruise, you will obviously not be in the moment. You will be surrounded by the thoughts of the next day's work back at home.

There is always a situation when you will be thinking about the future instead of living in the present. So life is all about enjoying the present and also taking care of our future.

Yes, everything matters in life. You need money for each and everything.

Are you planning for your child's marriage, have you arrived at an amount?

Are you planning to go for vacation each year, as you like travelling?

Are you planning to do an interior with automation, as you like being in a sophisticated environment?

All the above is just a common list. You can start adding more to your list. Did you notice that all these are future aspirations? Many people will have these aspirations. Only few who are working toward it will achieve everything in life.

> *"Money isn't everything in life but before saying that have a lot of money"*
> *- Anonymous*

Aspirations differ with people. A person who doesn't own a smartphone will not know about YouTube. You need to start planning your money for the following:

Healthcare

Your healthcare differs with your insurance or the money that you possess. This is a true incident that happened in a metro city. A man was getting frequent pain in his stomach area and the diagnosis was hernia. A hernia can be operated immediately. As he was almost bankrupt, he started enquiring about the price of the surgery in big and small hospitals. To his surprise one of the leading multi-chain hospitals across India, told him an exorbitant price, once he revealed that he is paying with his insurance.

With further investigation, it was evident that the price was only half of the price quoted. If he did not have this health insurance, then he would have had to pay for the surgery with his money.

Daily life
There are claims that the use of pesticides in crops has become the cause of cancer. Thus, organic vegetables, free of pesticides can avoid cancer, but you need to pay more for buying those products. The price of organic vegetables is almost double that of your existing groceries.

Therefore, even if you need better life, you need money.

Gadgets at home
Once you start buying one gadget, the others follow. It started with a mobile. You can control electronics like a fan, light, AC, with a mobile app. You can control your entire home with your mobile.

Now, you have host of devices like a smart TV, sound bars, projectors, sound system, etc. that can give you a theatre experience.

The best way to lead your life may be to embrace all the lifestyle changes you see.

Summary

1. Have a mean life or meaningful life
2. Luxury - it's not a big thing, we are already using it
3. Everything matters in life - being in the present and preparing for the future.

Action points

1. How are you leading your life?
2. Are you enjoying every moment and not worried about money?
3. If you are worried, take steps by following the previous chapters.

CHAPTER 10

Your Money Matters

Money, love, or anything in life grows only when you give it its due respect.

Do you know that the person who wins a lottery loses most of his money in seven or eight years? There can be exceptions for sure. Let's try to understand what happens with most of them.

The people who buy a lottery ticket believe in luck and spend a fortune on buying them. Once they win a lottery, most of them try to spend on things that were not available to them. Unable to match their new lifestyle, they lose everything in maximum eight years.

Let us discuss the story of my two friends. One is a miser who doesn't spend on things unnecessarily right from our college days. It was purely due to his family background. My other friend got used to anew lifestyle where he bought things on a whim over two months. He was the style icon in our office. The miser friend, tried to close his education loan and he came dressed modestly to office.

After two years, the miser friend increased his branding with an increase in his income. He also closed his education loan. The stylish friend was buying things with an EMI and he had added a personal loan to his existing education loan. So point here is that it is always wise to improve your lifestyle in a steady manner.

You need to improve your standard of living day by day. You can do that only when you identify your future aspirations.

Are you a *live in the moment* person?

You can ask, "Why should I think about tomorrow?"

Who asked you to worry about tomorrow? It's all about a careful allocation of your current income so that you don't need to worry during a tough situation.

Rahul and Shilpa got married. Even after four years, they used to save money and spend it on a vacation. They never thought of the future. They got a beautiful boy and it was a happy family. In one accident, Shilpa and Rahul met with some serious injuries. It took longer than expected for them to get well and he lost his job as well. This forced him to work in some company at a lesser pay to take care of the family.

Anything saved and invested would have been a relief during this period. It is all about saving and investing a portion for yourself.

Thought - mind - consciousness

Thoughts – using this you can bring anything you desire to life. Dr. Abdul Kalam had asked everyone to dream big and make it a reality.

Consciousness – this is the present state from where you think your thoughts and take the steps to make it happen.

Mind – this is the most intelligent part of human life. This helps in every moment to take a careful decision.

In your dreams, you dream about owning a Rolls Royce and having a luxurious home. When you see a Rolls Royce moving on the road, what are your conscious thoughts?

"This guy would have done some illegal business otherwise it is difficult to own this car."

Or other such negative thoughts pop up. If you say that you are happy for the person driving the car, then you are a rare person in this world.

Your thoughts differed from your consciousness and your mind knows this. You should be ready to train your mind to have your thoughts aligned to your consciousness.

The most difficult thing in this world is controlling your thoughts and channeling it in a way you want.

Creating wealth is easy once you align everything.

"Compound Interest is the eighth wonder of the world, and he who understands it… earns it. He who doesn't…pays it."

Einstein had rightly quoted this on money compounding.

Wipro, Reliance, and TCS shares created wealth over a period of ten years. Money compounds only in the long run.

Effective money management

Effective money management can easily help you in creating your own wealth.

> *"If you start buying things that you don't need, you will end up selling the things that you may need."*
> *- Warren Buffet.*

If you have money, you don't need to worry about the price while buying things. One thing you should check is, whether you really need it. It is difficult to do this after buying the commodity.

Prepare two lists. One is your buying list and the other is the avoidable list. List down all the shopping items in the buying list, right from groceries to all big purchases you have in mind to this list. Before going shopping, evaluate the highly priced items. Move those to the avoiding list temporarily. Check if it is necessary for you to buy now or can it be postponed by another three months. This way, you can postpone your buys for a while and it will become a habit for you.

S. No	Buy list	Avoid list
1		
2		
3		
4		

Are you having enough savings every month?

If you have dependents and other commitments in your life, you can still save a little every month.

Consider allocating a small portion as savings(Y) every month from your salary(X). Now your available income for expenditure is (X–Y), and with this you have just started money management.

In the next two years, if your income increases by 10 percent, it is the right time to analyze and solve all your money problems, with every increase in income.

Generally, it is not about how much you invest. It is about how committed you are to your wealth creation that matters.

> *"Starting small is very essential, rather than just ignoring it and waiting for more money in your life"*

Gratitude

Gratitude is nothing but saying thanks for what you have in your life. Only if you are grateful for your life, you can start to attract more positivity. Remember the *Mind, Thought, Consciousness* section where you need to be mentally aligned in order to create wealth.

The easiest way to get aligned is to start paying gratitude on daily basis. Every morning start practicing this. You will become happier and it is easier to attract your wealth.

To get to the next level in your life, you need to be happy about your situation. Only then can you work on the next step of creating wealth.

Conclusion

1. Make a list of your aspirations or goals in life. It can be owning a villa, retirement fund, bank balance, financial freedom, etc.
2. Start analyzing your monthly cash flow. Know your monthly savings ratio.
3. Be committed to have a minimum of 30 percent savings. If not increase it every month.
4. Start investing for your goals.
5. If there is no surplus amount left for investing toward all the goals, start prioritizing your goals.
6. Attaining financial freedom is a long process, keep monitoring and ask for help from an expert.
7. Make risk management plans for all your goals with correct insurance covers.
8. Have emergency funds to manage any situation.

You can go through all the above points, only when you have a mindset toward leading a prosperous life.

I hear people saying, "I don't have the money to invest, let me do financial planning later."

Wealth creation or financial planning, gives you a clear path to achieve wealth and financial freedom. Otherwise you will start investing in insurance as an investment product or you may invest in Ponzi schemes and lose your money.

Have everything in a common place

The most important thing is to have all the related documents in a common place.

1. All investment documents need to be in a common place
2. All insurance documents need to be in a common place
3. Note down the important dates with regards to renewal
4. Have a nominee name in all these documents
5. If needed write down a will
6. If you are married, all the details must be shared with your life partner

Summary

1. Save for tomorrow
2. Thought - Mind - Consciousness
3. Effective money management
4. Gratitude
5. How to approach wealth creation
6. Have everything in a common place

Action points

1. Align your mind, thought, and consciousness to lead a rich and prosperous life.
2. If you are missing something, start from "Expenses and Savings" in your life.

Final Summary

Expenses and Savings - Identify and acknowledge your expenses to start saving. It is the one and only way to create wealth.

Insurance - Manage your life risks even before choosing investment products.

Investment - Identify your needs and goals to choose an effective investment product that is suitable for you.

Loans - Use it wisely to manage your life, or else it will start controlling you.

Lifestyle - Everything is for improving and enjoying your life, so start managing your money effectively.

All the above five are needed to make your financial planning. Instead of financial planning, it has been mentioned as five leaks which when arrested can increase and improve your life drastically.

You may not be able to do everything together if you are just going to start. Identify the part that needs immediate focus and then make overall progress over a period of time.

Interviews

Murali Srinivasan

National Director, BNI India.

Murali Srinivasan is the National Director of BNI India. In the last few years, he has travelled across India attempting to open several chapters of BNI. He has rich experience of interacting with businesspeople in India, and it is a real honor to have his views on entrepreneurship, money, and personal finance.

In your view, how are entrepreneurs investing in India?

I have seen very few people investing. I classify people into three categories.

1. Survivors

    They are close to 40 to 50 percent of the population. They do everything on an ad hoc basis and will always be in survival mode.

2. Stabilizers

   They constitute 40 to 50 percent of the population. Here, people invest based on tips, and they don't have long-term vision for wealth creation.

3. Abundance

   Only 5 percent reach this stage, and then they think about investing.

How about the need for insurance

Term insurance is the most essential. All others come after this. Everyone should remember that **insurance is not an investment**.

How about your view on Gen X or Millennials?

It is not about Gen X, Gen Y, or Millennials. Everyone needs structure. Only if structure is there can they take care of their personal finance. They need to know about their earnings and how much they should save for their future.

Do you think a vision is necessary for business?

People should have vision, and they should be ready to sell their business while starting. Only then will business start flowing in.

Do you think a vision is necessary for personal finance too?

Even with personal financial, you should have vision. Otherwise, you will never invest or look into your future financial needs.

What will happen if financial structure is not there?

If financial structure is not there, everything will be done on an ad hoc basis. Most businesspeople are confused between business and family because they don't have the right structure.

Do you think there is need for financial advisors?

If you are not aware of something, you will go to an expert. Similarly, you can go to an expert to understand and structure your personal finance.

"Vision should be there for your business as well as for your personal finance"

CavinKare Ranganathan

Mr. CK Ranganathan is the Founder Chairman & Managing Director of CavinKare. A pioneer of innovation, Mr. CK Ranganathan has shaped the company to create innovative products by combining the best of nature and technology to improve the lifestyle of consumers. Under his inspiring leadership, the company, while expanding into personal care, also diversified into food, beverages, dairy, snacks, and salons both in domestic and international markets.

What is the best advice you can give to business people?
You take care of your people, and they'll take care of your business. Provide the right Vision, Values, and Goal and see them achieve.

What is your advice for startups or people who are entering business? Is business so risky to start?
Business is not rocket science. If you have the following four things, the chances of success are very high.

1. Abundant common sense
2. Good Emotional quotient
3. Business acumen
4. Leadership

Don't get too worried about not having money. I believe in Dr. Robert Schuler's quote "Nobody has money problems. It's idea problems."

Also, you should have the mental fortitude that even if you lose, you can rise up from the ashes and succeed.

One solid advice for all business people

"Invest in yourself" is the one solid advice I would like to give. Only this can pave way for growth and success. Daily, spend time alone in educating yourself. I observe solitude for two and half hours every morning between 5.30 a.m. to 8 a.m. I do the following things in that time: 1. Visualize one portion of my business vividly, 2. Reflect on yesterday as to how well I could have spent my time and what are the learnings, 3. Preparing for the day's goal and for each meeting of the day, 4. Reading or listening to relevant books where I need to enhance my knowledge to perform my job better, and 5. physical exercise.

How do you see people who mix personal and business income together?

There are two kinds of businesspeople… the first kind run their business like a "Family Business." For such people, family is first and the business is second. They will not hesitate to take money from business for family's pleasure and avoidable needs. They'll do this at the cost of their business. The second kind is called "Business Family." For them, business is like a temple, and they believe that if business is healthy then the family will be automatically taken care off. They'll never do anything that will harm the business, and they are extremely disciplined. They won't allow inefficient family members to spoil the business and will keep them away. They have a clear demarcation between ownership and management.

I designed my business as a "Business Family," and I will never harm the temple, which is my business.

Lot of businesses go up in flames as the promoters give priority to family's extravagant financial needs at the cost of the business's health.

How did you manage your personal finance earlier on?
I never used to take money at the cost of my business's health at any time. I withdrew salary on a monthly basis and learnt live within that.

I bought my own house after 20 years only after the business's needs were fulfilled like having our own space for office and R&D etc. At that time, my turnover was INR 350 crores.

My salary is my source of income then and even now.

What are the initial challenges you faced in your business?
My initial challenges were attracting talent, making my team believe in my vision, and getting finance to fund its growth. But with smart ideas, I could overcome these challenges.

Your ability to grow the business is directly dependent on team members with the right attitude. There are two kinds of people: growth mindset people and fixed mindset people. The growth mindset people will give ideas to grow and break the obstacles, while the fixed mindset people will refuse to change and will tell you reasons why it's impossible. They will magnify obstacles and will refuse to adapt to the emerging needs. I am happy that I had identified growth mindset people from the start.

What do you suggest for saving and investing to business people?
Financial discipline is the most important aspect of doing business. You should be capable of paying your employees for at least twelve months even if business becomes zero. The business must have at least such reserve money. The most fundamental thing is paying them well and on time. Also, if you take loans from banks or financial institutions, you need to pay the same on time or else you will not be able to get a loan for the second time.

I got my first loan of 25,000 only after three years. I got an increase on the loan without giving collateral security just because I used to pay income tax regularly and correctly. Banks respect income tax paying companies and are willing to go the extra mile if they're confident about repayment. Though I was small at that time, I paid my taxes regularly. My auditor advised in the beginning that I and my company must pay taxes correctly. This is how I started building my business.

Have you built any other asset?
I bought my first home only after twenty years, and I am very happy that I had the discipline at that age itself. Even my family was happy with the way we developed. My family lived within our affordable limits. I never borrowed for my family needs except for buying a property after 20 years. My kids studied based on the affordability at that time. I didn't go beyond my means at any point in time.

If you succeed in business, your assets will grow automatically. Even now, my family's important asset is our business.

Nowadays, I am not interested in real estate. In my opinion, the growth rate in these kinds of assets has reduced significantly.

Why do you invest in business?

I invest only in business nowadays because the returns are much more attractive than elsewhere. If your business grows well, you should invest only in your business. I am comfortable investing in intellectual properties because the returns are huge.

Would you advise going to a financial advisor for new entrepreneurs?

I welcome going to financial advisors. When you earn more money, you can spread your assets in personal finance.

What's your take on lifestyle?

"Live within your means." Don't borrow and spend for enjoyment.

Enjoy life all the time but within your affordable boundary.

What are the most important things in business?

Vision, Values, Goal, and Attitudes are the most important things for running any business. If your value system is good then you will bring in stability in your business.

You should have people with the right attitudes and have growth mindset people at leadership positions to grow the business even if the economy is not positive.

I follow the "Strategy, Structure, and People" model to run my business.

Strategy defines how to achieve your goals. To execute the strategy, you need the right structure. Structure is the competencies required and the kind of organization structure required to run your business. Finally, you should have the right people at the right job to execute the strategy. Brilliant strategy will be poorly executed if you don't have the right structure. Similarly, despite brilliant strategy and the right structure, the strategy will be poorly executed if you have wrong or mediocre people at various positions. Even one wrong person at a critical position can spoil the sport.

I want to share a quote that has worked well for me and many successful people:

"Whatever you vividly imagine, ardently desire, sincerely believe, and enthusiastically act upon must inevitably come to pass."

By Paul J. Meyer

FREE BONUS

Download your "Action Guide" for FREE

Thanks for your interest in arresting Money Leaks in your life. It can happen in any of these stages as mentioned in the book -

Expenses & Savings, Insurance, Investment, Loans, Lifestyle

Once you identify were your leak is happening,
it is easy to take actions.
We have provided an easy way to identify those money leaks.

Yes, all you need to do is
CLICK the below link and download the Action Guide.

http://www.ganesanthiru.com/ActionGuide

You will be on the path to "Financial Freedom"

About Success Gyan Publishing

We believe that everyone has knowledge to share and lessons to teach and what better way to do so than through a book.

Success Gyan Publishing, a publishing house formed with the mission to bring out the creative genius within everyone, aims to simplify the book publishing process for those who wish to share their knowledge through books.

Earlier, if you were to write and publish a book, you needed an agent to get a publishing house to look at your manuscript and even then there was no guarantee that they will publish your book.

Now, if you're wondering if there's a better way, there most certainly is. You can now take control of your book and how it is published through the Success Gyan Publishing platform. From planning your book cover to setting a timeline, the SGP team makes this daunting journey to becoming an author.

We are on a mission to help business owners and professionals to bring out the book in them, and help them transform their business or profession, by becoming an author.

Website - www.sgpublication.com
Email - info@successgyan.com

www.ingramcontent.com/pod-product-compliance
Lightning Source LLC
Chambersburg PA
CBHW030648220526
45463CB00005B/1678